False Friends in Business English

Stephanie Shellabear

HAUFE.

Contents

Vorwort

Ein „falscher Freund" (engl. false friend) ist ein Wort in einer Fremdsprache, das genauso oder ähnlich klingt oder geschrieben wird wie ein Wort in Ihrer Muttersprache, aber eine andere Bedeutung hat. Deshalb ist ein false friend nicht der korrekte fremdsprachliche Begriff. Wenn Sie false friends im Gespräch oder im Schriftverkehr benutzen, kann dies unterschiedliche Folgen haben: Muttersprachler mit guten Deutschkenntnissen werden in der Regel wissen, was Sie eigentlich sagen oder schreiben wollten. Sie werden Sie aber nur korrigieren, um Missverständnissen vorzubeugen oder Sie davor zu bewahren, sich lächerlich zu machen. Häufig sprechen Ihre Geschäftspartner jedoch kein Deutsch – und werden durch false friends in der Regel ziemlich verwirrt sein.

Und Vorsicht: Es gibt sehr viele false friends! Dieser Taschen-Guide zeigt Ihnen die wichtigsten, zunächst anhand zahlreicher typischer Business-Situationen – von der Bewerbung über den Small Talk bis zur Verhandlung. Auf diese Weise können Sie sich die korrekten englischen Begriffe besser einprägen. Eine umfangreiche Liste der false friends dient Ihnen als ständiger Begleiter zum schnellen Nachschlagen.

Ich wünsche Ihnen viel Spaß beim Entdecken der echten Freunde!

Stephanie Shellabear

False friends for beginners

When it comes to doing business, you always need to be prepared. If you are doing business in English, but your mother tongue is German, then you need to be prepared for the traps that the English language holds for you.

The following chapter will provide you with information about:

- the different kinds of false friends (page 6),
- the effect on your business contacts of language errors (page 8),
- typical mistakes in CVs, applications and interviews (page 9).

Different types of false friends

Same or similar word but different meaning

Take the German word *Mappe*. 'Map' exists in English but, while you are talking about something to put papers in, your English-speaking business contact thinks you mean a large piece of paper with roads and towns on it (*Landkarte*). The correct English word for *Mappe* – in this particular case – is 'folder'. Other examples are Gift/gift, Kredit/credit, Fabrik/fabric. You will find a list of the more frequently heard false friends in the latter half of this book.

Same or similar word and similar meaning

These are words that generally mean the same, but it depends on the context. Here is a standard example: *extra* and *Extra-*. If you say in German *Ich habe es extra so hingestellt, damit du es sofort siehst*, you would need to say in English 'I put it there deliberately so that you would see it'. If you are in a restaurant, though, and order *eine Extra-Portion Gemüse* you can say in English 'an extra portion of vegetables'. There is one verb which deserves special mention here, because it is probably the most frequently made mistake, namely: *machen/make*. We make mistakes, we make coffee, we make a fuss, but we do sports, we do courses and we do the accounts.

Via direct translation

You probably already know not to describe an *Unternehmer* as an undertaker, unless of course that particular entrepreneur or business owner really is an undertaker (*Leichenbestatter*). Similarly, it is widely known that a *Hochschule* is not the same thing as a high school.

Pseudo-anglicisms

These are English words that have found their way into everyday German usage but mean something completely different to the original English word, such as *Handy, Peeling* and *Body*. Others, such as *Wellness* and *Neckholder*, do not even exist in English; and some can shock your audience or perhaps make them laugh although you meant to be serious: take *public viewing*, for instance, which until now meant solely *öffentliche Aufbahrung (einer Leiche)*! It is better to talk about a 'live transmission on a big screen'. Who knows, perhaps these terms will gradually find their way into everyday English.

Non-existent English words

There is a strange phenomenon which occurs with just a few German words. They are often translated by German speakers into words that do not exist in English. One false friend of this type is *reservieren*, which many express as 'reservate'. 'Reservate' does not exist, but it is said automatically by many people due to what they have learnt so far of the English language.

Only a false friend in certain contexts

Take the German word *isoliert*: if the context is a location that is far away from anywhere else, then the translation is indeed 'isolated'. However, this is a false friend if we are talking about buildings and stopping the heat escaping from them; in this context you need to speak of 'insulation'.

Degrees of confusion

How disappointed or confused (or perhaps shocked!) will your conversation partner or email recipient feel if you use a false friend? The answer is: it depends. It depends on the word itself, and on how tolerant your opposite number is of hearing mistakes. It also depends on whether the person you speak or write to has any knowledge of German. The less German they know, the more potential there is for misunderstandings.

The cringe factor

Below is a simple scale to show you how other speakers of English, but especially native speakers, may feel when they hear mistakes made by (other) non-native speakers. These signs will help you to see how critical the use of a false friend can be, and it will hopefully help you to recognize which things you need to pay particular attention to:

↓ small error; it can cause some confusion,

↓↓ more critical; potential for big misunderstandings,

↓↓↓ don't say this: it may cause shock or embarrassment!

Applying for a job

There is no denying it: English is everywhere. If you are searching for a new job, it is likely that you will see under the list of requirements for the position: *gute* (or perhaps *hervorragende*, maybe *verhandlungssichere*) *Englischkenntnisse*. What sort of things should you be aware of when you apply?

Example 1: letter of application containing false friends

Dear Sir/Madam

I am applying for the job of photograph which you advertised in the Daily Times on Friday 3 September 2010.

Enclosed is my CV. You will see that I started to study to become an advocate, but I discovered a love of cameras and decided to become an undertaker instead and started up my own photo studio ...

What needs improving?

- The German word is *Fotograf* and the English for this is **'photographer'**. This applicant has just described himself as a photo. ↓

- An advocate is someone who supports, for example, an idea, e.g. 'he is a strong advocate of renewable energy'. It is not the same as *Advokat*, which in English is **'lawyer'** or **'attorney'**. ↓↓
- If only the English for *Unternehmer* were undertaker – life would be so easy! An undertaker is, as already mentioned, *Bestatter*, and the word the applicant should have used is **'entrepreneur'** or **'business owner'**. ↓↓↓

Example 2: letter of application with some false friends

> Dear Sir/Madam
>
> I have been following the developments of your company for a while now with great interest. It is my wish to work for a globally successful company and so I am sending you my CV in case you actually have a vacancy for someone with my qualifications.
>
> I was an executive assistant in the direction of a medium-sized German company for three years and am a very engaged team worker. My former chief was very satisfied with me and I am enclosing the reference that he wrote ...

What needs correcting?

- The German adverb *aktuell* and the English 'actually' are very similar but they mean different things. *Aktuell* translates as **'currently'**. The English adverb 'actually' means *eigentlich*. ↓
- The applicant says she worked 'in the direction', which means *in der Richtung ...* What she should have written

was, for example, **'in the office of the board of directors'** or **'at head office'**. ↓↓

- Last but not least we have the classic false friend *Chef*. Although there are titles such as 'Chief Accountant' (*Hauptbuchhalter*) and 'Chief of Staff' (*Generalstabschef*), 'chief' also means *Indianerhäuptling*! The correct translation for *mein Chef* is **'my boss'** or **'my manager'**. ↓

Example 3

Dear Ms Terry

With regard to your announcement in the Good Thinking magazine on 15th January I would like to apply for the job of Sales Assistant.

I enclose my CV which shows that I have worked in the sales resorts of several companies. I read about your fusion with Alex plc and I am sure that a fresh and competent face in your sales department will bring your company many benefits ...

What's not right?

- Announcement. *Annonce* is so similar to this. However, 'announcement' means *Ankündigung*. The correct thing to say in the case above is **'advertisement'**. ↓
- We speak of 'holiday resorts' in English (*Ferien- / Urlaubsort*) but not of sales resorts or personnel resorts. The right word for this is **'department'**. ↓↓
- The applicant mentions a 'fusion' of Alex plc and the company she is writing to. Does she know that she has used

the translation of *Verschmelzung*? The word that describes the joining together of two companies is **'merger'**. ↓

Useful vocabulary

catch on	Schule machen; sich durchsetzen
recipient	Empfänger
opposite number	Gegenspieler; Verhandlungspartner
cringe	schaudern

Your CV

This is an interesting challenge: trying to fit the details of a large part of your life on just one or two pages. That is why it pays to get it right first time. There is not much you can do wrong with your personal details, but things like your education and work experience need a little care.

Example 1: CV containing false friends

Education

1992 - 1994	Promotion in Business Administration, University of Bayreuth
1987 - 1991	Diploma in Business Administration, University of Bayreuth
1979 - 1986	Unting Gymnasium

Be careful!

- When you talk or write about the achievements in your educational history, do find the correct translation. The English word 'promotion' means *Beförderung* in German. The qualification you gained was in fact a **'doctorate'** or **'PhD'**. ↓↓
- 'Diploma' is a universal word. It can be used for all kinds of qualifications after various lengths of study and/or work experience. If you studied for several years at a university, though, it is safe to call your final qualification a **'degree'**. ↓
- Do not say you went to school at the 'gymnasium'. That is the hall in which you do sports activities and exercise (*Sporthalle*). You can choose between **'secondary school'** and **'high school'** to refer to *Gymnasium*. ↓↓↓

> Did you know that 'bachelor' also means *Junggeselle*? Say 'He's got a bachelor in Chemistry' or 'He did his bachelor's in architecture two years ago'. If you say 'He's a bachelor', you might need to explain whether you mean he has this qualification, or that he is unmarried.

Example 2: CV containing false friends

Employment

01/2009 - date	Expanded company into Austria – overtook **WeWillDesign**. Now Managing Director of three companies
12/2008	Built second company **Olidesign**, specializing in floors
01/2005	Grounded and led own decorating company **Außen.Innen** with German state's existence grounding money
01/2003 - 12/2005	Apprenticeship as decorator

Is s/he or isn't s/he?

The information in this CV is **confusing** (*irritierend*) not: 'irritating').

- Let us start with the oldest piece of information: 'decorator'. Does this person mean 'decorator' as in *Maler/Tapezierer* or perhaps **'interior designer'** (*Dekorateur*)? ↓
- The next thing we see is that this person **founded** (not 'grounded' – *aus dem Verkehr ziehen*) his own company. ↓
- *Leiten* is sometimes 'to lead' but in this context it is better to write **'managed (my) own company'**. ↓
- The *Existenzgründer* support is better explained as a state grant given to people to set up their own businesses. *Existenz* in this case is not 'existence' but **'one's own company'**. ↓↓

- *Bilden* is a verb you see often, but it is better translated as **'to form'**. You can build a **factory** (*Fabrik*) but you **form** (or **found**) a company. ↓
- Does the company Olidesign specialize in floors (*Böden*) or **hallways** (*Flure*)? ↓
- Lastly, 'to overtake' means *überholen*. It is better to say **'took over** WeWillDesign', or better still: **'acquired'**. ↓↓

> If you really want to get the job you are applying for, ask someone with excellent English – someone who knows you well – to check your CV before you send it. As the English saying goes: better safe than sorry (*Vorsicht ist besser als Nachsicht*).

The interview

Has an interviewer ever tested your English during a German interview? Or have you attended an interview that was held entirely in English? Some people love to demonstrate their knowledge of a foreign language and have no trouble speaking with confidence. Nevertheless, look out for false friends!

Some typical questions

Here are just a few of the types of question you will be confronted with in interviews. What is wrong with the answers?

Why would you like to work for us?

- Even before I absolved my study I wanted to work in the financial branch. ↓
- Your concern has such a great reputation all over the world and that is why I am so interested. ↓↓
- The marketing ideas that you create are genial and I want to be a part of that. Yours is a very representative company. ↓↓

What experience could you contribute to this job?

- First and foremost my experience in great, successful companies: I am calm even when there is a lot of hectic in the office. I can stay focused under pressure. ↓
- My biggest hobby is cars. I've spent my whole life with them and I have several Oldtimers at home. You won't find anyone as passionate about them as me - and I can use this momentum to achieve a lot at work. ↓↓↓
- Because we have a family business, I have always spent weekends and holidays working there. Over the years I have learned a lot about loan accounting, sales, advertising and personal. ↓↓

What do you do in your spare time?

- I am doing a part-time study in translation. The next exam is in two weeks, so I am spending most of my evenings learning at the moment. ↓

- I enjoy reading in my free time. I like all kinds of different lecture. ↓
- I make a lot of sport. In the winter I go skiing, and in the summer I like wandering in the mountains. ↓↓

What's wrong?

Did you work out which statements are not correct? Here they are, one after the other. Notice the differences and try to memorize them for future use.

This was said:	But this was meant:
absolve *freisprechen*	passed; got *absolvieren*
study *Arbeitszimmer*	studies; degree *Studium*
concern *Sorge*	corporation, enterprise *Konzern*
genial *gesellig*	brilliant *genial*
representative *repräsentativ für etwas*	prestigious *repräsentativ*
great *großartig*	large *groß*
hectic *hektisch*	a lot of activity *Hektik*

This was said:	But this was meant:
old timer *alter Hase*	antique car; vintage car *Oldtimer*
loan *Kredit*	salary; payroll *Lohn*
personal *persönlich*	personnel, human resources *Personal*
learning *lernen*	revising (for a test or exam) *lernen*
lecture *Vortrag*	reading material; books *Lektüre*
make sport *Sport schaffen*	do sports *Sport machen*
wandering *umherwandern*	hiking *Wandern*

False friends in business communication

If you are going to talk to someone on the telephone, write an email or a letter, participate in a meeting, present to a group of people, or handle negotiations of some kind, it is a good idea to watch out for the language pitfalls illustrated in this chapter.

The following chapter contains numerous false friends hidden in

- a phone conversation (page 20),
- two types of written correspondence (page 21),
- presentations, and a face-to-face conversation (page 25).

On the telephone

Telephone conversations with English-speaking business contacts can be a challenge. You cannot see those tell-tale facial expressions (rolling of eyes, frowns of confusion, or smiles of amusement) that would normally indicate whether you have said the right thing in English.

Example

Joachim calls his colleague John who is located in his company's British subsidiary.

Joachim: Hi John, it's Joachim here. Am I calling at a good time?

John: Hi Joachim, how are you doing? I've got a couple of minutes before my next meeting. What's it about?

Joachim: Nothing serious! I wanted to ask you if you're coming to the trade fair in London in two weeks. Can we have a date?

John: Pardon? ↓↓↓ *(John wonders if he should warn Joachim that he has just told him he wants a romantic rendezvous with him).* Do you mean can we arrange to meet up? Yes, I'll be free all day on the Wednesday. How are the preparations going?

Joachim: As usual everything is last minute. We are still waiting for the prospects to arrive. You can't go to a trade fair without prospects to give to people.

John: But the prospects are what you are going there to collect, aren't they? ↓↓ *(John does not realize that Joachim is talking about brochures. Prospects are potential customers that companies go to trade fairs to impress.)*

Joachim: I don't understand what you mean, but anyway, we will be ready on time. I hope you will be able to spend a few hours with us at the booth. There will be a special feature: a tour of one of our fabrics using virtual reality. The visitors won't need to use their fantasy because the experience will feel completely real.

John: Yes, I can imagine. It sounds interesting. Tell you what, as soon as I get to the exhibition centre, I'll come and find you and we can arrange a time to go off and have a chat. *(John is a little confused now because Joachim has talked about walking round a fabric – Stoff – and using a fantasy – einen Traum. Joachim should have said 'factory' and 'imagination'.)* ↓↓

Joachim: OK. Bye John!

What is the cringe factor of this conversation? It could be rated as an overall ↓↓.

Whatever you do, avoid using 'date' unless talking about a private, romantic type of meeting or, of course, a specific day. Everything else is an **appointment**.

In emails

Email is a means of communication with extra risks. It can be hard to get across in just a few words what you mean. If your email is going to be sent to everyone in your company – or even to external contacts or customers, your false friends could make a poor impact, at least on native English speakers.

Find the false friends

Example: email containing false friends

From: M. Prohl
To: All employees
Sent: 30 May 2010
Subject: Summer feast

> Dear colleagues,
>
> we heartily invite you to our summer feast 2010!
>
> You all know the company tradition of a summer feast and many of you have already attended it over the years. This time, we have a special occasion to celebrate – the 10th birthday of our company. So the celebration will be a little bit different and certainly more special.
>
> Please registrate yourself using the following link if you can attend and later you will become an armband in the internal mail which you will need to enter the event.
>
> We will send you more information soon. Until then, the device is "let's have some fun!"
>
> Many greetings,
>
> Melinda

This email contains an array of entertaining false friends: entertaining for native speakers, that is, if they know a lot of German. Let us start at the top and take each one of these false friends in turn.

What's wrong?

- The first incorrect term is 'heartily'. You should not translate this directly. Instead, use the phrase 'You are **cordially** invited to ...'. ↓↓
- Next comes 'summer feast', clearly originating from *Sommerfest*. Feast means *Festmahl* in German: a focus on eating (lots!); but what we are looking at here is a **summer party**. ↓↓
- Have you ever said 'registrate yourself' or perhaps 'reservate (a table)'? If you ask English teachers whether they have heard their pupils – native German speakers – say

this, many of them will say yes. The words 'registrate' and 'reservate' do not in fact exist, though you would be forgiven for thinking they did. Say **'register'** (it is not reflexive) and **'reserve'**. ↓

- Bekommen/become. They are practically the same, but so very different in meaning. We often hear 'I became a present', *ich bin ein Geschenk geworden*. This mistake has the potential to be embarrassing, so remember to use **'receive'**. ↓↓↓
- So, after registering to attend the summer party you will receive an armband: *einen Schwimmflügel* (in British English)! It also means one of those wide fabric bands that a soccer team captain wears around the upper part of his/her arm during a match. This type of entrance ticket to big events and parties is better described as a **'wristband'**. ↓↓
- If you want to say *die Devise ist ...*, don't say the 'device is ...' (*das Gerät ist ...*), use **'the motto is'** instead. ↓↓↓
- 'Many greetings' is not the English form of *viele Grüße*. Write 'Best regards' or 'Kind regards' instead. ↓

Tips for emails

- Just as in letters, the first line after the greeting should start with a capital letter.
- Use a spell-check function before you press send.
- If your email is important and intended for an international list of recipients or for customers, ask a native speaker to proof-read and correct it first.

In letters

We tend to communicate mostly by email, text message and telephone these days. However, letters are not yet extinct.

Example: letter containing false friends

Dear Mr Todd

Thank you for your letter dated 10 February 2010.

We want to say a hearty thank-you to you for the allowance to display your painting in our house during our 10th anniversary celebration. The painting represents very strongly the engagement of our staff and it is thanks to them that our company is so successful.

I enclose opera cards for you and your wife to enjoy an evening out together, as a token of our thanks.

With best regards ...

What needs correcting?

This was written:	But this was meant:
a hearty thank-you *ein deftiges Dankeschön*	many thanks; a warm thank-you *ein herzliches Dankeschön*
allowance *Taschengeld*	permission *Erlaubnis*
in our house *in unserem Haus*	at our premises *in unserem Hause*

This was written:	But this was meant:
the engagement of our staff *die Verlobung unseres Personals*	our staff's commitment *das Engagement unseres Personals*
opera cards *Opernspielkarten*	opera tickets *Opernkarten*

In meetings

Do you tend to spend the majority of your time in meetings? It may help to learn a few phrases off by heart and avoid false friends that way. Can you spot any mistakes in the phrases below? Not all of them contain errors, by the way.

Typical phrases in meetings – with false friends

- Hello everyone.
- Shall we start?
- Can I ask you to write the protocol?
- The meeting will end at 5pm. We'll have a short pause at 3.30 for coffee and cakes.
- Have you all got a copy of the agenda?
- Can anyone let me have a sheet of paper? I've left my block in my bureau.
- The first item on the agenda is ...
- So that's the situation. What is your meaning?

- Barbara, do you want to begin?
- Does everyone share that opinion? If not, what is the ground?
- Are there any disagreements?
- I don't completely agree. We all have different arguments.
- Could I just say something? I'm sure we can arrange ourselves.
- I'd like to just point out that eventually ...
- Sorry to interrupt but I need to mention here that ...
- Can I just finish what I was saying?
- Shall we return to the main issue?
- Let me summarize what we've just agreed upon punctually.
- I'll make a notice that the deadline is ...
- The date for the next meeting is ...

The sentence above contains the word 'date'. In this case it is completely correct because this time it is about *Datum* and not *Termin*.

What is the correct term?

Don't say this:	Say:
write the protocol *die Benimmregeln schreiben*	write/take the minutes *das Protokoll schreiben*
a pause *eine Atempause*	a break *eine Pause*

Don't say this:	Say:
cakes *Kuchen*	biscuits/cookies *Kekse*
block *Klotz*	notepad *Block*
bureau *Amt*	office *Büro*
What is your meaning? *Was ist Ihre Bedeutung?*	What is your opinion? *Was ist Ihre Meinung?*
What is the ground? *Was ist der Boden?*	What is the reason? *Was ist der Grund?*
arguments *Streitigkeiten*	points of view *Argumente*
arrange ourselves *sich ordnen*	come to an arrangement *sich arrangieren*
eventually *schließlich*	perhaps *eventuell*
punctually *pünktlich*	point by point *punktuell*
a notice *ein Aushang*	a note *ein Notiz*

Do you keep your meeting agendas, papers, notes, and perhaps business cards, a notepad, and a pen in a medium-sized, flat object that you normally carry under your arm or in your hand? What would you call it in English? Many German speakers are tempted to call it a 'map', because of the German term *Mappe*. If you ask an English speaker 'Is it ok if I put my map down here?', he or she will think you want to put on the table a very large piece of folded paper showing towns and roads: *eine Landkarte*. The word you need is **'folder'**, or **'file'**, or if it is made of leather: **'briefcase'**.

Making presentations

For natural performers, this is a chance to shine. But for the less confident among us – especially where English is concerned – this can be a daunting situation. See what effect these typical false friends have.

Better phrases for presentations

Avoid saying this:	Say this instead:
Good morning everyone. I want to say how lucky I am to be here today. *... was ich für ein Glück habe, heute hier zu sein.*) ↓↓	Good morning everyone. I'd just like to say how great it is to be here to talk to you today. *... wie glücklich ich bin, heute hier zu sein.*
The theme of my presentation is ... *Die Titelmelodie / Das Motiv meiner Präsentation ist ...* ↓	The subject of my presentation is ... *Das Thema meiner Präsentation ist ...*

Avoid saying this:	Say this instead:
First, I will talk about ...; next I will tell you about ...; and last I will give you some stuff to think about. *Zuerst will ich über ... sprechen und als nächstes will ich Ihnen über .... erzählen. Zum Schluss will ich Ihnen etwas Zeug zum Nachdenken geben.* ↓↓	Firstly, I'd like to talk about ...; then I'll go on to tell you about ...; and finally I'd like to provide you with some food for thought. (*Ich will* and 'I will' are often used as if they were identical, but of course they are not. 'I'd like to' has a better ring to it – it shows that you are taking your audience into consideration.)
Can we move the beamer a little? It blends in this position. *Können wir den BMW ein wenig umpositionieren? So wie er steht, mixt er.* ↓↓↓	Could we move the projector a little? It's shining right in my eyes at this angle. *Können wir den Beamer ein wenig umpositionieren? So wie er steht, blendet er mich.*

If you are showing an unfinished presentation to your colleagues with information that you plan to change soon, do not write on it 'To be overworked'. It could be that you were overworked when you wrote the presentation (*Sie waren überarbeitet*) but the correct text is 'To be updated' (or 'revised' or 'amended').

Negotiating

Negotiating is all about two sides reaching an agreement. Watch out for false friends and make sure that your wishes are understood.

Example: Negotiation containing false friends

Holly: Hello, Pia. Come in and have a seat.

Pia: Thanks. Holly: So, what did you want to talk to me about?

Pia: I know we normally talk about these things in the yearly evaluations, but they are not for another six months.

Holly: Go ahead.

Pia: Because the theme is important to me, I wanted to talk to you sooner about becoming a salary raise. I have been in the department for five years and my pay is still the same. This is relatively low for our branch when you think of the work that I do and my engagement.

Holly: I can understand your situation. However, business was bad the last two years and we are now only just beginning to increase turnover again. We aren't quite out of the woods yet.

Pia: Yes, I understand about the conjuncture. But I would like to see my performance paid at the market price. Inflation has increased in the last five years, too, also I am earning less than at the start, though I work harder.

Holly: My hands are tied where money is concerned. I can't allocate any more for salaries until the evaluation round. What I can do at present, though, is offer you other concessions ...

Which false friends were used?

- Pia spoke about a 'theme' that was important to her. As already mentioned, in this context it is better to say **'subject'** or **'topic'**. ↓
- Pia wants 'to become a salary raise' (*sie will eine Gehaltserhöhung werden*). This mistake happens a lot and can be forgiven, but it certainly confuses English speakers with no knowledge of German. Use **'to have'** or **'to receive'**. ↓↓↓
- Another common error is using 'branch' as a translation of *Branche*. You can talk about the Frankfurt branch of a German company (*die Frankfurter Filiale*) but otherwise say **'sector'** or **'industry'**. ↓↓
- 'Engagement' was also mentioned earlier. It is not Pia's *Verlobung* that she should be emphasizing, but her **commitment**. ↓↓↓
- Also/*also*? Be careful here. '... also I am earning less ...' should be '... **so** (or **therefore**) I am earning less ...', because Pia is pointing out a consequence. ↓

Tips for negotiations

- Write down on paper the things you want to talk about, your point of view and the reason(s) for it. Check it before your meeting.
- If you are not used to conducting negotiations in English, look up the vocabulary you are not sure about beforehand – online dictionaries are a good resource if they provide

example sentences to show the correct use of words that have various meanings.

Useful vocabulary

in turn	der Reihe nach
pitfall	Falle
tell-tale	verräterisch
an array of	eine Vielzahl
text message	SMS
extinct	ausgestorben
off by heart	auswendig
daunting	beängstigend
out of the woods	aus dem Gröbsten raus

False friends on a business trip

Do you travel often? Here are some of the situations you are most likely to encounter on a business trip. Maybe there are a few things in this section that you will have the opportunity to try out right away.

In this chapter you will see some false friends in action:

- at the airport (page 34),
- at a restaurant and while shopping (page 36),
- and when small talk takes place (page 42).

At the airport

The check-in staff at international airports can usually speak at least one other foreign language, so checking-in is normally easy, especially now it is more automated. Still, watch out for false friends, whether you are an airport employee or a business traveller.

Example

Lisa has arrived safely in Manchester, but her luggage has not.

Lisa: Hello, my coffer hasn't arrived. Is there someone who can help me?

Baggage claim attendant: Coffer? *(The man smiles. He knows 'a coffer' as a wooden box full of treasure that pirates normally search for.)* What does it look like?

Lisa: It's big, blue, and it has rolls.

Baggage claim attendant: *(understands: groß, blau und hat Brötchen! Looks at the empty baggage carousel.)* No, it doesn't seem to be here. Do you see that office over there? The lady in there can help you.

Lisa (in the office): Hello, my coffer has not arrived. Do you know where it is? Here is my pass, and here is my boarding pass from the machine I came in.

Employee: *(Wonders what type of machine Lisa travelled with – normally air passengers travel by plane.)* Aha, I see. I'll look in the computer and perhaps we can locate your luggage. I see it was just one suitcase, am I right?

Lisa: Yes, that's correct. I knew something would go wrong. We started an hour late and ... this is really a problem.

Employee: I'm afraid the database has no record yet of the whereabouts of your suitcase, but I expect it will be updated any moment. When it arrives, we can have it delivered to you. Could you tell me where you are staying?

Lisa: But what will I do until my suitcase arrives? All my things are in it ...

Employee: I can give you a voucher so that you can buy the essentials, and I am certain you will have your case by this evening.

Lisa: I see I have no choice. I will give you the address of my hotel and my handy number.

Employee: *(understands: nützliche Telefonnummer)* Thank you; that would be great.

What needs to be corrected?

Don't say this:	Say:
coffer *Truhe*	suitcase *Koffer*
rolls *Brötchen*	wheels *Rollen*
pass *Bergpass; Eintrittsschein*	passport *Pass*
machine *Maschine/Gerät*	plane; flight *Maschine*
start *beginnen*	take off *Start*
handy *handlich*	mobile/cell phone *Handy*

At a restaurant

There are some clear winners among the false friends that show up in restaurant talk. At some time or other you will be eating together with English-speaking colleagues or customers, be it lunch, an evening meal or even a business breakfast. Look at the phrases below and see if you can work out the mistakes.

Typical phrases in restaurants – with false friends

- Hello. I reservated a table for four people under my name: Gold.
- Could you bring us the cards, please?
- What is the menu of the day?
- We'd like two bottles of water – one with gas and one without gas.
- Excuse me, I have become the wrong beer – I ordered alcohol-free.
- Is the Thai curry very sharp? Can I have it with crabs?
- I would like my steak English, please.
- Could you bring some more sauce for the beef, please?
- I would like the 'warm apple strudel' for dessert. Does it come with vanilla sauce?
- (And last but not least when paying the bill) Where do I underwrite?

What's not right?

- German speakers very often say 'reservate' for *reservieren*. 'Reservate' was mentioned earlier and does not exist: it is a strange type of false friend that is said automatically by German speakers of English. You need to say **'reserve'**. ↓
- 'Card' has several different uses, but if you mean *Speisekarte*, say **'menu'**. ↓↓
- That takes us to *Menü*, which is known as **'daily special'** or **'dish of the day'**. ↓↓
- 'With/without gas' is understood easily in most countries when you order in English. If you want to sound less like you are asking for water with or without *Erdgas*, ask for **'sparkling'** or **'still water'**. ↓
- 'I have become the wrong beer' – *ich bin das falsche Bier geworden*. This has the potential to make your waiter or waitress grin widely because it sounds so funny. Could this be the number one false friend? Remember: *bekommen* is **'to receive'** or **'to get'**. ↓↓↓
- *Krabben* are called **'prawns'**. Crabs are those large, pink crustaceans with dangerous claws. ↓↓
- 'Sharp' is good for describing things like knives, people's intellect and lemons. If you are talking about curry, you should say **'spicy'** or **'hot'**. ↓↓
- 'Sauce' is too unspecific in English when it comes to food. If you mean *Fleisch-* or *Bratensoße*, say **'gravy'**. *Warme Vanillesoße* is called **'(hot) custard'**.

- And now to the bill/check: 'underwriting' is the job of insurers; when you receive the credit card printout in a restaurant, you **sign** it.

Tips for visits to restaurants

- Often, it is not so much what you say in a restaurant that is important but how you say it. Although it is accepted in German restaurants to motion to the waiter and discreetly say 'We'd like to pay', in English it is more polite to say 'We'd like the bill/check now, please'.
- Although this is not really a false friend, *Garderobe* is translated by some as 'wardrobe' (*Kleiderschrank*). The correct word for the place you leave your coat is the 'cloakroom', or a 'coat stand' or 'coat rack'.

When shopping

If you have reached your destination but your luggage has not, perhaps you need to buy a few essentials. Or maybe you have a day or two free in between meetings and have a shopping trip on your to-do list. Read on and take note of potential false friends.

Better phrases for shopping

Clothing is a subject in which there are many false friends. Several terms started to appear in German not so long ago that really do not mean the same thing in English. However, as mentioned at the start of this book, some things have been accepted into English now, even though they did not exist before. If, in the past, you had said in a clothes shop 'I'm looking for a red body to go with my outfit', the sales assistant's face would have been a picture! *Ich suche einen roten Körper, der zu meinem Outfit passt.* This piece of underwear used to be called a **'teddy'** – and it still is, but nowadays the term **'body'** is indeed used.

'Overall' is a good false friend: if you say this in English it will be understood as *Schutzanzug* or *Blaumann*. The correct name for this, if it is a piece of fashionable clothing that you are talking about, is **'jumpsuit'**.

The word *neckholder* does not exist. You need to use the term **'halterneck'** instead.

An amusing case of direct translation has to be 'hand-shoes'. You need to say **'gloves'** *(Handschuhe)*.

Please note that if you ever need to talk about the following things, be careful. There is potential here for a high cringe factor! In British English, 'slip' means *Unterrock*, and 'vest' means *Unterhemd*. If you need to talk about *Unterhosen* – one never knows! – women's are called 'pants' or 'panties' and men's are called 'underpants'. In American English, 'pants' are *Hosen*, so simply use the term 'underwear' if it's something you wear *drunter*.

With clothing, avoid:	Say this instead:
I am going to a prize event this evening and I need a smoking. *Heute Abend gehe ich zu einer Preisverleihung und brauche dafür ein Rauchen.* ↓↓	I am going to a prize-giving event this evening and I need a dinner jacket (BE)/tuxedo (AE). *... und ich brauche dafür einen Smoking.*
Is there a vest with this jacket too? Der Brite versteht: *Gibt es dazu ein Unterhemd?* ↓↓	Is there a matching waist-coat (BE)/vest (AE) for this jacket? *Gibt es zu diesem Sakko/ dieser Jacke eine passende Weste?*
Excuse me, I want to buy a jeans-jacket. Do you sell these? *Entschuldigen Sie, ich will eine Jacke aus Jeans kaufen. Haben Sie so was?* ↓↓	... I'd like to buy a denim jacket. Do you sell them? *... ich möchte eine Jeans-jacke kaufen.*
Hello, I need some help. I'm looking for some slippers. *Guten Tag, ich suche Pantof-feln.* ↓↓	... I'm looking for some cas-ual shoes/loafers. *Guten Tag, ich möchte ein Paar Slipper.*

Other things to avoid:	Say this instead:
Excuse me, where is the next warehouse? *Entschuldigen Sie bitte, wo ist die nächste Lagerhalle?* ↓↓	Excuse me, could you tell me where the nearest department store is? *Entschuldigen Sie bitte, wo ist das nächste Warenhaus?*
I want to buy a liquor to take home as a gift. Can you show me something typical or traditional for here? *Ich will eine Spirituose/ Alkohol als Geschenk für zu Hause kaufen. ...* ↓↓	I would like to buy a liqueur ... (You need to pronounce this as lik-ior. Liquor is pronounced likker.) *Ich möchte einen Likör als Geschenk kaufen.*
Marmalade is always a good present. What sorts do you have? *Zitronenmarmelade ist immer ein gutes Geschenk. Welche Sorten haben Sie?* ↓	Jam is always a good present. Which types do you have? *Marmelade ist immer ein gutes Geschenk. ....*
Excuse me, where's the cash? I want to pay for these things now. *Wo finde ich das Bargeld, bitte? Ich will diese Sachen bezahlen.* ↓↓	Excuse me, where will I find the till/ the check-out counter? I would like to pay for these things now. *Wo finde ich die Kasse? ...*

Other things to avoid:	Say this instead:
This cup is a gift for my mother. Please could you pack it in a carton because I'm taking it back to Germany in my suitcase. *Diese Tasse ist ein Geschenk für meine Mutter. Könnten Sie sie bitte in eine Tüte tun, weil ich sie nach Deutschland zurücknehme?* ↓	This is for my mother. Please could you pack it in a box because I'm taking it back to Germany in my suitcase (and I don't want it to break). *Diese Tasse ist ein Geschenk für meine Mutter. Könnten Sie sie bitte in einen Karton tun, ...*

Small talk

Is small talk the big, bad wolf of business English? Many non-native speakers are certainly afraid of it. Small talk is important for creating long-lasting business relations and for making a good impression in social circles. If you do not practise, you cannot improve, but before you dive right in, do take note of some more of those typical false friends.

Phrases for business situations

It's relatively easy to say hello to someone and ask how he or she is doing. Here are some less obvious phrases that are useful to know in business situations.

Example 1

Birgit has just arrived at her company's office in the UK.

Birgit: Hello, I have a meeting with Mr Johnson at 14 hours. I am sorry I am late. I went to the wrong stock: 32 instead of 23.

Receptionist: *(Understands the mistake 'stock' because Birgit mentioned the floor numbers).* It's ok. I will call him and tell him you're here. Please have a seat while you're waiting.

Birgit: Thank you. There was a little hectic today because my machine from Hamburg fell out and I had to fly one hour later.

Receptionist: *(Confused about what it means when a machine falls out.)* Here's Mr Johnson now.

Birgit: Mr Johnson, hello!

Bill Johnson: Hello! Please, call me Bill. It's Birgit isn't it?

Birgit: Yes. It's nice to see you. I have some blooms for you because I heard it is your birthday today. Congratulations!

Bill Johnson: *(Hears the small mistakes, but understands and does not correct Birgit.)* Thank you very much, what a nice surprise!

How do we really say it?

- 'Stock' means *Lagerware*. The correct word for the numbered levels in a building is **'floor'**. ↓↓
- You can say **'things were a little hectic'** but not 'there was a little hectic', because this word is an adjective in English, not a noun as in German. ↓
- Birgit's 'machine fell out'. Non-German speakers will be scratching their heads over this. The correct phrase is **'my flight was cancelled'**. ↓↓↓

- Taking a gift to someone who has a birthday is a kind gesture, but 'blooms' are better described as **'flowers'**. 'Blooms' are *Blüten*. ↓
- The correct greeting for someone with a birthday is '**happy birthday**'. 'Congratulations' sounds almost ironic – almost like 'it's great that you made it through another year'! ↓↓↓

Although it is usual to say the afternoon and evening times in German using 13, 14, 15 etc, it is not said like this in normal everyday English. Any time after 12.59 in the afternoon should be expressed as '1pm, 2pm, 3pm' and so on.

Example 2

Birgit is back at reception at the end of her day in the UK.

Birgit: We've finished our meeting now. Could you help me find a taxi?

Receptionist: Oh I can call you one. It will only take 10 minutes for it to arrive.

Birgit: Great. I need it to bring me to my pension. Oh dear, look at my costume! I spilled sauce on myself at lunchtime. That's typical of me.

Receptionist: *(Is smiling politely, but is getting distracted by the strange English she's hearing).* It doesn't look bad. I am sure the mark will come out easily.

Birgit: I have a free day tomorrow. Can you recommend any-where to visit? I'm not a city person – I like to be in the nature, but I have heard there is a beautiful dome near here.

Receptionist: That's right. I have a brochure here if you're interested. There is a concert taking place there tomorrow

evening. My husband is playing in the orchestra.
Birgit: That sounds good. I love classic music.

What can be improved?

- Birgit wants a taxi to bring her to her pension – *ein Taxi, das sie zu Ihrer Rente bringt.* She needed to say **'to take me to the guesthouse I'm staying at'**. ↓↓↓
- She spilled sauce on her costume – *verschüttete Soße auf Ihre Verkleidung.* It is no wonder that the receptionist was beginning to get confused. To be precise, she **spilled gravy on her suit.** ↓↓↓
- She likes to be 'in the nature' (**'outdoor's** or **'in the countryside'**) and wants to visit a 'dome' (*Kuppel*) – though she clearly meant a **'cathedral'**. ↓↓
- Last but not least, Birgit loves classic music – *Klassiker* – though she no doubt means '**classical** music'. ↓

Useful vocabulary

whereabouts	Verbleib
voucher	Gutschein
essentials	Lebensnotwendige
grin	grinsen
underwrite	garantieren
motion to sb.	jemandem ein Zeichen geben
matching	passend
denim	Jeansstoff
to mingle	ein Bad in der Menge nehmen

False friends in different departments

So far you have been seeing some situational examples of false friends used in English. This chapter takes a different perspective and deals with the functionally relevant false friends: those that crop up in some of the different departments of a company.

The following situations will show you typical false friends that can occur in the departments of:

- human resources (page 48),
- logistics (page 50),
- finance and accounting (page 52),
- sales and marketing (page 54),
- and production (page 55).

Human resources

One of the responsibilities of the HR department is to collaborate with other departments in the preparation and writing of job descriptions.

Example

An HR assistant has received some information about a vacant position from a colleague and has translated it into English for the job description.

Job description	Examples
Job title:	Leader of IT
Reports to:	Company direction
Start date:	As soon as possible.
Advertising of vacancy:	Internally and announcement in national newspaper.
Stand-in:	Colleagues
Objectives of this function:	Development of department according to company's actual goals. ...
Responsibilities:	Controlling the department's processes and implementing methods of improvement. Cooperating with leaders of other departments to optimize IT's services. ...
Professional requirements:	IT study at university. Five years experience in a similar position. Great and sovereign knowledge of standard office IT systems. ...
Personal requirements:	Excellent analytical skills. Excellent communicator. Because of different nationalities in teams must be sensible to different cultures. ...

What needs to be corrected?

This was written:	But this is meant:
leader *Führer*	head (Head of IT) *Leiter*
company direction *Firmenrichtung*	company management *Direktion*
announcement *Ankündigung*	advert *Annonce*
actual goals *tatsächlichen Ziele*	current goals *aktuelle Ziele*
controlling processes *Prozesse steuernd*	examining processes *Controlling-Prozesse*
IT study at university *Studieren der IT an der Uni*	university degree in IT *IT-Studium an der Uni*
great and sovereign knowledge *großartige und adlige Kenntnisse*	wide-ranging, expert knowledge *große und souveräne Kenntnisse*
sensible *vernünftig*	sensitive *sensibel*

You may already have seen some of these false friends in the other sections of this book. The alphabetical list of false friends in the second part of this book contains (page 58) many more examples which relate to a range of different business and personal areas.

Logistics

If your goods and/or services are supplied physically to the customer, then the main purpose of logistics is to deliver those goods and services to their destination without delay.

Effective communication is therefore of paramount importance.

Example: email containing false friends

Jürgen is still waiting for a consignment of office furniture that he ordered for his company two months ago.

From: Jürgen Mann
To: Jeff Jones
Sent: 25.11.2010
Subject: Reclamation - Order Number 5789614

Dear Mr Jones,

This is about our order of ten desks and ten office chairs on 20 September 2010.

Last Monday I spoke on the phone with your lager. I told them that the furnitures had not arrived yet. They controlled all our order dates and said they knew what had happened. They told me that the furnitures were on the way to our city by train but a wagon was defect.

They said I should become everything yesterday but nothing has arrived.

Please could you find out where our furnitures are and call me with informations as soon as possible, because my colleagues do not want to work on the floor!

Thank you.

Regards,

Jürgen Mann

What's not right?

This was written:	But this is meant:
reclamation *Rückgewinnung*	complaint *Reklamation*
lager *helles Bier*	warehouse *Lager*
control *steuern*	check *Kontrolle*
order dates *Bestelltermine*	order data *Bestelldaten*
become *werden*	receive *bekommen*

It is incorrect to say 'furnitures' and 'informations' in English. Neither of these terms has an s at the end. The plural forms are simply **'furniture'** and **'information'.**

Finance and accounting

If you work in the finance department of a large, international company, perhaps you have a lot of contact with colleagues in offices in different parts of the world, and no doubt English is your company language for all communication with these colleagues.

Example: phone conversation containing false friends

Julio is Spanish and works in accounting in the London office of a global company. Kirsten is a German colleague working in the company's Frankfurt office.

Kirsten: Hello Julio, it's Kirsten from the Frankfurt office. How are you?

Julio: Hello Kirsten, fine thanks. How are you?

Kirsten: A bit stressed. I'm calling to ask about a booking on one of our cost centres that was done in the London office. We are making an internal revision at the moment and the controller wants to know more details about the post.

Julio: (*Wonders what is being changed internally. In addition, he is accustomed to hearing the term 'Controller', though in Britain, people in these jobs are called 'management accountants'.*) So it's about some post? Was it a courier delivery? We normally only charge big amounts to projects if they are higher than 100 pounds, otherwise the amount goes straight to general administration costs.

Kirsten: No I don't mean post like sending letters; I mean the booking that was made on the cost centre. It is for 2000 pounds.

Julio: A booking? Do you mean a reservation? Perhaps it's to do with an event then. Can you tell me the cost centre code and the month and I will look at it in the system.

Kirsten: It's ACY24.60 and it was July. But it isn't a reservation, it's a real booking.

Julio: Do you mean a charge that was entered?

Kirsten: Yes, that's right.

Julio: Oh, now I understand. You know what? If you email me a pdf of the report showing the charge, I will call you back as soon as I have the information you need.

Kirsten: That would be fine. Thank you Julio.

What caused the confusion?

- Strictly speaking, 'a booking' is something you make when you want hotel rooms, concert tickets or tables in restaurants. Also, footballers can receive bookings from the referee, meaning they are shown the yellow or red card for fouling other players during a match. When talking in German about a *Buchung* in an accounting system, in English it is more specific if you can say **'an entry has been made'** or **'a debit has been charged to'** or on the positive side: **'an amount has been credited to'**. ↓↓
- An 'internal revision' sounds like changes being made within the company, whereas in this case an **internal audit** is taking place. ↓↓
- The correct accounting term for *Posten* is not 'post' but **'item'**. ↓↓

One of the terms that can often confuse native English speakers is the German speaker's use of the term 'controller' and 'to control'. It gives a sense of *die Macht haben über etwas/jemanden*, but in the financial context it is usual to say **'management accountant for'** *Controller* and **'to monitor/to check'** for *kontrollieren*.

Sales and marketing

Not so long ago, German companies such as car companies, perfume sellers and cosmetics manufacturers began marketing their products and filming adverts (*Spots*) with English slogans. With time, some of them have realized that the non-English speaking population often do not understand the message; so they have reverted to using German slogans.

The most amusing situations – for native speakers of English, that is – arise from German companies using pseudo-anglicisms to name their products. Here are some examples:

Product name in German:	What the English speaker understands:
Shirty (a type of nightdress)	'Shirty' is used to describe a person and means *aufgebracht*.
Shorty (pyjamas with short trousers)	'Shorty' is a nickname often given to people who are not very tall: *Kleine(r)*.
Body (name given to one-piece underwear: one type worn by women and a type also made for babies)	'Body' means *Körper*. The kind worn by women is typically known as a 'teddy' but, as mentioned earlier, it is also now called a 'body' in stores in Britain. The type worn by babies is called a 'babygrow' (BE) or a 'onesie' (AE).

Product name in German:	What the English speaker understands:
Bodybag (a ruck-sack with a single strap that lies di-agonally across the front of the body)	Bodybag means *Leichensack*. This is not a good choice for your product name!
Neckholder (a piece of clothing with straps which are tied behind the neck)	'Neckholder' *(Nackenhalter?)* does not exist. The correct English ex-pression is 'halterneck', e.g. hal-terneck dress, halterneck top.

This is not simply a recommendation: it is a necessity. If you wish to use English words to name, describe or advertise your products and/or services, it is crucial that you have them checked for their meaning in all of the English-speaking countries in which you hope to sell them.

Production

This is the division (*Ressort*) that manufactures products; it is the place where your ideas, in the form of designs, are turned into reality. In this context it is acceptable to speak of your concepts being 'realized' (*realisiert*).

Example: a meeting dialogue containing false friends

At a product team meeting, three colleagues of different nationalities are updating each other on the status of the production of a plastic kitchen utensil. They are Hannes from the *Konstruktionsteam*, Melinda from *Materialentwicklung* and Sam, a native English-speaking product manager.

Sam: ".... as I was saying, we're having one main issue with the product and I was hoping we could start analyzing it by going back to the source. Hannes, the main difficulty we are having is with this section of the product *(Sam points to a diagram)*. As an engineer, perhaps you can see immediately what we need to improve."

Hannes: "You know I am not an engineer really, but I see the problem and I think that the construction needs to be improved at this place here ..."

Sam: "OK, I see – but so that we all understand this correctly, we're talking about the design, right? The construction is the building of the product."

Hannes: "Oh, you're right, yes, the design. We need to make a change to this part of the product, make it thinner."

Melinda: "But I am not sure if the material will still be as strong as before. If you make this part thinner, the product could break more easily and that would mean a lot of reclamations."

Sam: "Reclamations? What do you mean exactly?"

Melinda: "When customers are angry about the product breaking and want their money back."

Sam: "I see. You mean complaints."

In Germany, only people who have an engineering degree are permitted to call themselves engineers. Native English speakers use the term less strictly: the people who come to repair your washing machine, your TV, your fridge or your freezer can all be called an **'engineer'** or a **'technician'**.

Tip

It is normally very rare for native speakers to correct other people's English, because they do not want to create any embarrassment or cause you to feel insulted. If it does happen, then it is probably because the situation is very important and it is necessary to make certain that there is absolutely no confusion. In cases such as these you should make a note to remind yourself of your mistake.

Useful vocabulary

to crop up	auftauchen
of paramount importance	von größter Wichtigkeit
consignment	Lieferung

Useful false friends to know

If you mean...	say this:
This...	**means:**
absolvieren	to pass; to complete* He passed his exams with flying colours. They have all satisfactorily completed the software course.
absolve	*freisprechen*
Advokat	solicitor (BE) / lawyer** She has just qualified as a lawyer.
advocate	*Verfechter; Befürworter*
Aktion	campaign It was a very successful advertising campaign.
action	*Handlung; Bewegung*
aktualisieren	to update The statistics have now been updated.
actualize	*verwirklichen*
aktuell	current What is the current situation in banking?
actual	*tatsächlich; Ist-*

* Words which are separated by a semi-colon have different meanings.
** Words separated by a slash have similar meanings and can be used as synonyms for each other.

If you mean... This...	say this: means:
alarmieren	to alert Please alert the police in the event of theft.
alarm	*in Angst versetzen; erschrecken*
also	well / so Well, if you really want my opinion ...
also	*auch*
Ambulanz	outpatients' (department) She's waiting in the outpatients' department to have her arm x-rayed.
ambulance	*Krankenwagen*
amüsieren, sich ~	to enjoy oneself We really enjoyed ourselves at the theatre.
amuse	*belustigen; amüsieren*
Angina	tonsillitis He's off sick with tonsillitis.
angina	*Herzschmerzen*
annoncieren	to advertise The vacancy is advertised in this week's newspaper.
announce	*ankündigen; verkünden*
apart	elegant / stylish That's a very elegant suit you're wearing!
apart	*abseits, entfernt*

If you mean... This...	say this: means:
Argument	point I'm not sure I understand your point. But: The arguments for and against a change.
argument	*Streit; Auseinandersetzung*
arrangieren, sich ~	to come to an arrangement They've finally come to an arrangement about who will take over the job.
arrange	*ordnen; sortieren*
Arrest, unter ~ sein	to be detained He's being detained and I don't know why.
arrest	*verhaften; festnehmen*
Art	type / kind / sort; nature This type of product sells extremely well. It's not in his nature to complain.
art	*Kunst*
Artist	performer She's an excellent performer.
artist	*Künstler/in*
ausfallen	to be cancelled My meeting was cancelled this morning.
fall out	*herausfallen*

If you mean... This...	say this: means:
ausmachen	to represent These statistics fully represent our clients' opinions.
make out	*ausstellen; dahinter kommen; darauf kommen*
Band	volume; recording; ribbon This is the 3rd volume in the series. We have a recording of the whole conversation. I'd like a ribbon tied around the gift, please.
band	*Kapelle; Gruppe; Streifen*
Bank	bench; riverbank We waited outside on a bench. The spectators watched the boat race from the riverbank.
bank	*Bank (Geldinstitut); (Fluss-)Ufer*
Basis, (~-)	grass-roots; basis We need a grass-roots approach to this issue. But: We used the statistics as a basis for our decisions.
basis	*Fundament; Ausgangspunkt*
Beamer	(multi-media) projector I need a projector to show my presentation.
beamer	*BMW*

If you mean... This...	say this: means:
bekommen	to receive / to get I received a letter today from the tax authorities.
become	*werden*
beliebt	popular This type of advertising is very popular.
beloved	*(heiß)geliebt*
bilden	to form Have you formed a plan yet?
build	*bauen*
Billion	thousand million (BE) / trillion (AE) How many trillion dollars have they lost?
billion	*Milliarde*
Biskuit	sponge cake This dessert consists of sponge cake and cream.
biscuit	*Keks*
blamieren	to make a fool of oneself / to embarrass oneself She made a complete fool of herself.
blame	*beschuldigen*

If you mean...	say this:
This...	**means:**
blank	shiny / bright Whose shiny, new company car is that? But: Never give anyone a blank cheque!
blank	*unbeschriftet; Blanko~*
blenden	to dazzle / to blind The light is blinding me. I need to move.
blend	*mischen; vermengen*
blinken	to indicate You need to indicate before you turn left!
blink	*blinzeln*
Blinker	indicator Do you know your indicator is still on?
blinker	*Scheuklappe*
Blitz	lightning That plane was hit by lightning in 1998.
blitz	*Blitzkrieg*
Block	notepad / writing pad Could you pass me a notepad, please?
block	*Klotz*
Blume	flower Those flowers are beautiful! Is it your birthday?
bloom	*Blüte*

If you mean... This...	say this: means:
Box	loudspeaker We need bigger loudspeakers in here.
box	*Kiste; Karton*
Branche	sector / industry I work in the insurance sector.
branch	*Filiale; Ast*
brav	well-behaved / good I agree; their children are very well-behaved.
brave	*tapfer*
Brief	letter All the information you need is in this letter.
brief	*Kurzdarstellung; Kurzanweisung*
Brillant	cut diamond His company trades in cut diamonds.
brilliant	*glänzend; großartig*
bringen	to take; to bring Shall I take this parcel to the post office now? I'll bring the report when I see you tomorrow.
bring	*bringen*

If you mean...	say this:
This...	**means:**
Büro	office She won't be in the office until this afternoon.
bureau	*Amt; Unterabteilung*
Buchung	debit/credit entry There's a debit entry on my cost centre that I don't agree with.
booking	*Reservierung; Verwarnung (Fußball)*
checken	to realize I didn't realize that she was the boss!
check	*kontrollieren; überprüfen*
Chef	boss I'll introduce you to my boss. But: Who is the current US Chief of Staff?
chef / chief	*(Chef-)Koch; Häuptling*
City	town Shall we travel into town together?
City	*Londoner Finanzdistrikt*
Controller	management accountant; cost controller You need to be a qualified management accountant to apply for this position.
controller	*Lotse; Kontrolleur; Steuergerät*

If you mean... This...	say this: means:
Controlling	cost control I work in cost control.
controlling	*Steuern; Überwachen*
Daten	data; dates Here are the final data from our survey.
dates	*Verabredungen; Kalenderdaten*
Datum	date What's the date today?
date	*Rendezvous; Tagesangabe*
defekt	out of order / not working The photocopier is out of order.
defect	*überlaufen; Störung*
definitiv	definitely We are definitely going to attend the event.
definitive	*endgültig*
Dekorateur	interior designer; interior decorator He's an interior decorator. She's studying to become an interior designer.
decorator	*Maler*
delikat	sensitive; subtle This is a sensitive subject. This dish has a very subtle lemon flavour.
delicate	*zerbrechlich; zart*

If you mean... This...	say this: means:
Delikatesse	delicacy Which dishes are considered a delicacy in China?
delicatessen	*Feinkostgeschäft*
dementiert	denied The boss has denied all knowledge of this matter.
demented	*verrückt / wahnsinnig*
demolieren	to vandalize The shop was vandalized during the night.
demolish	*abreißen; vernichten*
desinteressiert	indifferent You seem very indifferent about this subject.
disinterested	*unparteiisch; unvoreingenommen*
Devise	motto I think our motto is clear.
devise / device	*ausdenken / Gerät*
dezent	subtle The message we're sending is very subtle.
decent	*anständig; ordentlich*
dick	fat / overweight More and more people are overweight.
thick	*dumm; dick (für alles außer Menschen)*

If you mean...	say this:
This...	**means:**
Direktion	head office / headquarters; company management He works at head office. She works directly for the company management.
direction	*Richtung*
Dissertation	thesis I wrote a thesis about bilingualism in children. But: What is your dissertation all about?
dissertation	*Doktorarbeit; dissertation*
Dom	cathedral Have you ever visited Salisbury Cathedral?
dome	*Kuppel*
Dusche	shower The shower in my room is not working.
douche	*Intimdusche*
einschlafen	to fall asleep I fell asleep on the train to Hamburg.
sleep in	*ausschlafen*
energisch	forceful He's always quite forceful in his opinions.
energetic	*energiegeladen; aktiv*

If you mean... This...	say this: means:
engagiert	committed My team is fully committed to achieving our company's goals.
engaged	*verlobt*
Erlaubnis	permission First you need to get your boss's permission.
allowance	*finanzielle Unterstützung/Taschengeld; Rücksicht*
Etikett	label Could you remove the label for me, please?
etiquette	*Etikette; Benimmregeln*
eventuell	perhaps / maybe / possibly It would perhaps be a good idea to sell it now.
eventually	*schließlich/im Endeffekt*
Evergreen	(golden) oldie They're using a golden oldie in their TV ads.
evergreen	*immergrüne Pflanze*
Exemplar	copy Could you send me a copy of the newsletter please so that I can check it?
example	*Beispiel*

If you mean...	say this:
This...	**means:**
Existenz	livelihood His whole livelihood depends on the success of his company.
existence	*Bestehen; Dasein*
extra; Extra-	especially; on purpose / deliberately I brought along this English newspaper especially for you. We dropped the price deliberately to see if it would increase demand. But: Please could you bring us an extra portion of fries?
extra	*zusätzlich; besonders*
Fabrik	factory We are going to build a new factory in Bavaria.
fabric	*Stoff; Gewebe*
Falte	wrinkle; crease We are going to start producing a new anti-wrinkle cream. My shirt is all creased from the long flight.
fold	*Falte (Papier~); falten*
familiär	domestic / family He has resigned for family reasons.
familiar	*vertraut; bekannt*

If you mean...	say this:
This...	**means:**
Fantasie	imagination She doesn't have a very active imagination, unfortunately.
fantasy	*Fantasiebild*
faul	lazy I've been very lazy this week. But: Where is that foul smell coming from?
foul	*widerlich; übelriechend*
fehlen	to be missing/absent; to be lacking Three colleagues are absent today due to illness. Our ideas are lacking something, but I'm not sure what exactly. But: Words fail me. I don't know what to say.
fail	*durchfallen*
Fehler	mistake / error There's an error in that formula. Let's check it.
failure	*Misserfolg*
Fest	party We are throwing a big party to help Chris celebrate his retirement!
feast	*Festmahl*

If you mean... This...	say this: means:
fixieren	to stare; to locate Everyone was staring at me; I don't know why. I couldn't locate which part of the machine the noise was coming from.
fix	*reparieren*
flattern	to be in / get into a flap He really got into a flap about that email.
flatter	*schmeicheln*
Fleisch	meat What do we call the meat from deer? But: Don't worry; it's just a flesh wound.
flesh	*Fleisch*
Flirt	flirtation It was just a brief flirtation, nothing more.
flirt	*flirten; Flirt (d.h. Person)*
Flocke	flake The snowflakes were enormous.
flock	*Herde*
Flur	hallway Please leave your coat in the hallway.
floor	*Boden; Stockwerk*

If you mean... This...	say this: means:
Folie	film; transparency / slide We are developing a new type of coated film that can be removed without leaving marks. You can see our sales figures on this slide.
foil	*Metallfolie*
Form	shape Our machines can produce any shape you want.
form	*Formular*
Format	dimensions; stature Is it possible to manufacture the same product according to different dimensions? He is a man of stature. But: Can you print this in the same format?
format	*Format*
Formular	form Please could you fill in this form? Thank you.
formula	*Formel*
Fotograf	photographer She's a photographer by trade.
photograph	*Foto*

If you mean... This...	say this: means:
Fraktion	parliamentary group; faction It's a parliamentary group for animal welfare. They belong to a very liberal faction of the party.
fraction	*Bruchteil*
Fusion	merger After the merger they changed the firm's name.
fusion	*Verschmelzung; Zusammenschluss*
Gasthaus	restaurant; inn Have you tried the small Italian restaurant next door yet? Let's go to that little inn on the outskirts of town.
guesthouse	*Pension; Gästehaus*
genial	brilliant That's a brilliant suggestion!
genial	*freundlich; gesellig*
Genie	genius You're a genius – that's a great idea!
genie	*Dschinn / Flaschengeist*

If you mean...	say this:
This...	**means:**
Gift	poison You sell rat poison? Oh!
gift	*Geschenk*
glücklich	happy I'm very happy to be here today.
lucky, to be ~	*Glück haben*
Grad	extent; degree (°C, °F) We can only service the equipment for free to the extent of our warrantee. The temperature in Athens today is 30°C.
grade	*Note; Qualität,(Schul-)Klasse*
Gratulation	Congratulations! Congratulations on your promotion! But on birthdays: Happy birthday!
congratula-tions	*Gratulation!; Herzlichen Glückwunsch!*
groß	large / big I work for a large company in France.
great / gross	*großartig / ekelhaft*
größte/r/s	largest / biggest Our company is the largest in the world.
greatest	*beste; großartigste*

If you mean... This...	say this: means:
Grund	reason That's the reason why I cannot attend today.
ground	*Boden; Erde*
gründen	to found He founded the company 20 years ago.
ground	*Hausarrest erteilen; aus dem Verkehr ziehen*
gültig	valid My passport is only valid for two more months.
guilty	*schuldig*
Grüße	wishes Best wishes, Marla / Warm wishes, Megan But: Greetings from Munich! Simon
greetings	*Grüße*
Gurke	cucumber I'd like my salad without cucumber, please.
gherkin	*Gewürzgurke*
Gymnasium	secondary school; high school
gymnasium	*Sport-/Turnhalle*
halten	to keep Please keep the information confidential.
hold	*(fest-)halten*

If you mean... / This...	say this: / means:
handeln	to deal; to act What's the best way to deal with this problem? We have to act now if we want to see results. But: How do you want to handle this matter?
handle	*handhaben / behandeln*
Handy	mobile phone / cell phone My mobile phone has been stolen!
handy	*handlich*
Haus	office I'm sorry; he is not in the office today. But: I invited them to my house for dinner.
house	*Haus*
Hektik	rush You always seem to be in a rush. Take it easy!
hectic	*hektisch*
Helm	helmet You need to wear a safety helmet in the factory.
helm	*Steuer / Ruder*

If you mean... This...	say this: means:
herzlich	cordial; warm You are cordially invited to join us in celebrating ... With warm regards, ...
heart(il)y	*zünftig; tiefempfunden*
Hochschule	university; college I went to university in Birmingham, England.
high school	*Sekundarschule: Gymnasium, Realschule, usw.*
honorieren	to reward; to pay We would like to reward all the hard work you have done for us. How much are they prepared to pay for the work?
honour	*ehren; auszeichnen*
Hose	trousers The waiter spilled red wine on my trousers.
hose	*Gartenschlauch; Strumpfhose (AE)*
human	humane They are demonstrating for humane working conditions!
human	*Mensch; menschlich*

If you mean... This...	say this: means:
Hymne	anthem Can you sing your national anthem off by heart?
hymn	*Kirchenlied*
imprägnieren	to coat with / to spray with If you spray your shoes with this substance, it will protect the leather.
impregnate	*schwängern; imprägnieren*
irritieren	to confuse I was confused by my colleague's statement. But: I was a little irritated by his criticism.
irritate	*ärgern; reizen*
Jubiläum	anniversary The club will be celebrating its 20th anniversary this year. But: Do you remember the Queen's Silver Jubilee?
jubilee	*Jubiläum*
Kalender	diary; time-planner I'm not sure if I have time on Wednesday. Let me just check my diary. But: There's a calendar over there on the wall. Can you see what day of the week the 30th falls on?
calendar	*Kalender*

If you mean...	say this:
This...	**means:**
Kamerad	mate / pal Can I introduce you to Simon? He's an old mate of mine from my schooldays.
comrade	*Genosse*
Kanal	channel We don't receive channel TV where I live. We are too remote. But: Goods used to be transported around the country on the canals and waterways.
canal	*Kanal / Wasserstraße*
Kanne	pot; jug Could you pass me the coffee pot, please?
can	*Konservendose*
Karte	ticket I have tickets for a gospel concert on Saturday. Would you like to come along?
card	*Karton; Visitenkarte; Grußkarte; Ansichtskarte*
Karton	box Where will I find a box to put my files in?
carton	*Tüte; Schachtel*

If you mean...	say this:
This...	**means:**
Kasse	till; check-out Can you show me where the check-out is, please?
cash	*Bargeld*
Kaution	deposit; bail If you wish to take this apartment, you'll have to pay a deposit of three months' rent. The actor was allowed out of prison on bail.
caution	*Warnung*
Kissen, Kopf~	pillow Ask the flight attendant for a pillow and blanket. It'll help you to sleep. But: Our waiting area is not very comfortable. Let's buy some cushions for the seats.
cushion	*Sitzkissen*
klassisch	classical I enjoy listening to classical music.
classic	*Klassiker; klassisch*

If you mean...	say this:
This...	**means:**
kochen	to boil Water boils at 100°C. I'll make some coffee. But: My husband only cooks at the week-ends.
cook	*kochen*
Konfession	religious denomination This section of the form is where you need to tick the religious denomination you be-long to.
confession	*Beichte*
Konjunktiv	subjunctive I always had problems at school under-standing the subjunctive. You too?
conjunctive	*verbindend*
Konjunktur	economy The economy has suffered a lot lately but it finally appears to be recovering.
conjuncture	*Sachlage; Zusammentreffen*
konsequent	consistent It is important to maintain a consistent strategy.
consequent	*daraus folgend*

If you mean... This...	say this: means:
konstruieren	to design We have succeeded in designing a model which can be manufactured in one piece.
construct	*bauen*
Konstruktion	design This is an award-winning design.
construction	*Bau*
kontrollieren	to check It's my job to check the travel expense claims.
control	*steuern*
kosten	to taste You must taste this dish; it's superb.
cost	*Kosten*
Kostüm	ladies' suit You should wear a suit for your interview, Evelyn. But: My son wants a Spiderman costume!
costume	*Kostüm; Verkleidung*
Kraft	strength / energy I eat lots of fruit because it gives me energy.
craft	*Kunsthandwerk; Gewerbe*

If you mean... This...	say this: means:
Kredit	loan The bank has agreed to give us a short-term loan.
credit	*Guthaben*
Kritik	criticism; critique If you have any constructive criticism, we'd be happy to hear it. Try not to read a critique of the show you are about to see; it might spoil the experience.
critic	*Kritiker*
Lager	stockroom / storeroom; warehouse I will just check the stockroom for your size. Our warehouse is located a few streets away.
lager	*helles Bier / Lagerbier*
Land	country; state; countryside He's from another country, but I'm not sure which. Our headquarters is in the state of North Rhine-Westphalia. We have a cottage in the Welsh countryside. But: They've bought some land from a local farmer.
land	*Grund und Boden*

If you mean...	say this:
This...	**means:**
Landschaft	countryside; scenery Have you ever travelled by train through the English countryside? The scenery is breathtaking in certain regions. But: This part of the country is characterized by its agricultural landscape.
landscape	*Landschaft; quer*
Leiter	Head We have created a completely new position: Head of Quality Management. But: He is a very respected team leader.
leader	*Führer; Anführer*
Lektüre	reading matter; read I've picked up a lot of reading matter on this subject. I'll summarize it for you on Friday.This novel is an excellent read. I can highly recommend it.
lecture	*Vortrag*
lernen	to revise Sorry, I can't come out with you all. My accounting exam is in ten days' time and I need to revise for it. But: I would love to learn Japanese some day.
learn	*lernen*

If you mean...	say this:
This...	**means:**
Likör	liqueur This is a special Finnish liqueur; it is very sweet and has a strong liquorice flavour.
liquor	*Spirituosen; alkoholisches Getränk*
liquid(e)	(financially) solvent Her company is no longer solvent. They might have to declare themselves bankrupt.
liquid	*flüssig*
Lohn	wages / pay Their pay is supplemented by set amounts for overtime and work at weekends and on public holidays.
loan	*Darlehen*
Lust (haben auf)	to fancy Where do you fancy going for lunch today?
lust (to ~ after sth/sb)	*Begierde; etw./jdn. begehren*
Mann	husband I sometimes accompany my husband on his business trips. But: He's a very demanding man; he will keep you on your toes, believe me.
man	*Mann*

If you mean... This...	say this: means:
Mappe	folder I have all the documents we need in this folder here.
map	*Landkarte*
Marmelade	jam / jelly (AE) I think I will buy some jam from Harrods as a present for my sister.
marmalade	*Citrusmarmelade*
Maschine	plane; flight Our plane landed early. That doesn't happen very often. I missed the flight and had to take the later one. But: We will be presenting our new machine at the trade fair in two weeks.
machine	*Maschine*
massiv	solid All of the furniture we produce is made of solid wood.
massive	*riesig*
meinen	to think What do you think about our new financial strategy? But: No, that's not what I mean. Let me explain it a different way.
mean	*bedeuten*

If you mean...	say this:
This...	**means:**
Meinung	opinion We've heard everyone's opinions now. Shall we put it to the vote?
meaning	*Bedeutung*
Menü	set meal; daily special We've ordered a set meal for the evening event. But there will be a vegetarian alternative. I'd like the daily special please.
menu	*Speisekarte*
Mimik	facial expression Your facial expression tells me you aren't satisfied with my proposal.
mimic	*Imitator*
mobben	to bully We are having problems with bullying in the workplace.
mob	*umlagern*
Moderator	presenter / host; facilitator He's a TV presenter. His show is on at 8pm every Thursday. We have asked Harry to act as facilitator at today's meeting.
moderator	*Moderator; Bremssubstanz*

If you mean... This...	say this: means:
Montage	assembly My team is responsible for the machines' assembly and installation.
montage	*Bildmontage*
Moral	morale; ethics How do we effectively boost morale within the company? Team ethics will play a very important role in this particular project.
moral	*Moral*
Motor	engine He can fix anything with an engine: generators, ship's engines, car engines, you name it.
motor	*Motor; Auto*
nächste/r/s	nearest Hi, can you tell me where the nearest petrol station is? But: Who is presenting next? We're ready for them now.
next	nächste/r/s

If you mean...	say this:
This...	**means:**
Natur	outdoors; countryside There's nothing more relaxing than being outdoors, away from suburbia. But: I have a question of a private nature.
nature	*Natur*
neulich	recently I saw a documentary on the TV recently that was all about the effects on consumers of precisely this type of marketing.
newly	*neu(-)*
nobel	posh / fancy; classy I am not a fan of posh restaurants. I prefer something more down-to-earth. It's a very classy place. It'll be perfect for this year's Christmas party.
noble	*adelig; großzügig*
Note	grade / mark I never got good marks at school in maths. I was always bottom of the class.
note	*Notiz*
Notiz	note I'll make a note of that and check it when I am back at my desk.
notice	*Mitteilung; Anzeige*

If you mean... This...	say this: means:
Objekt	property We are currently looking for a new property to develop into office suites for small companies.
object	*Gegenstand*
Objektiv	lens The photographer is here somewhere. I think he went to look for a spare lens for his camera.
objective	*objektiv*
Oldtimer	antique car / vintage car We had a brilliant team event: a vintage car rally during the day and a cocktail party to round off the day.
old timer	*alter Hase*
ordinär	vulgar His uses very vulgar language. I will have to speak to him about it.
ordinary	*alltäglich; unauffällig*
Paar	couple Here's some office gossip for you: those two have been a couple since the summer party. But: I need a pair of brown shoes to match my suit.
pair	*Paar*

If you mean...	say this:
This...	**means:**
Paket	parcel / package Hello, Peter? Can you come to reception, please? There is a parcel here for you.
packet	*Packung / Schachtel*
Paragraf	section We would like to draw your attention to section C of the contract where we stipulate our terms and conditions.
paragraph	*Absatz; Paragraph*
Pass	passport May I see your passport?
pass	*Passierschein; Eintrittskarte*
pathetisch	emotional The managing director gave an emotional speech.
pathetic	*jämmerlich / miserabel; herzergreifend*
Pause	break OK, let's take a 15-minute break and then go on to point 3.
pause	*Pause*
Pension	guesthouse I decided to stay at a little guesthouse near the client's this time. I wasn't satisfied with the service at my last hotel.
pension	*Ruhestandsgeld*

If you mean...	say this:
This...	**means:**
per	by I sent the invoice last week in the post. Haven't you received it yet?
per	*pro*
Perlen	beads Are these real Murano glass beads? They're beautiful. But: I inherited these pearls from my grandmother.
pearls	*Perlen*
Personal	staff / personnel; human resources I have a meeting with my staff this afternoon. I'll give them the news then. He's head of human resources.
personal	*persönlich*
Plastik	sculpture In this exhibition you will see various sculptures from the German Renaissance era. But: All of these machines process plastic materials, whereas the other machines work with metal materials.
plastic	*Kunststoff*

If you mean... This...	say this: means:
Platz	square; seat I'll meet you on the main square in the town centre. Please have a seat.
place	*Ort; Stelle*
Pointe	punchline I was listening to him tell a joke, but there was an interruption so I completely missed the punchline.
point	*Punkt*
Police	policy Shall we discuss the insurance policy now?
police	*Polizei*
Posten	item; position I've checked the accounts and I need some explanation of the following items. He's been offered a new position within the department. But: He has resigned from his post as ecturer.
post	*Post; Pfosten; Stelle*
prägnant	concise I'd like a concise summary of the meeting.
pregnant	*schwanger*

If you mean...	say this:
This...	**means:**
Präservativ	condom In order to prevent the spread of HIV we recommend the use of condoms.
preservative	*Konservierungsmittel*
Preis	prize; price This year's winner of the architecture prize goes to ... The price of gold has increased tremendously.
price; prize	*Preis*
Probe	test; sample My son has an English test at school today. Would you like a free sample of our new perfume?
probe	*Sonde; Erforschung*
Programm	channel; schedule Our company will be featuring in a documentary on Channel 3 this evening at 9pm. Can we keep to the schedule, please? But: I bought a programme when I was at the theatre yesterday. Would you like to borrow it?
program(me)	*Programm*

If you mean...	say this:
This...	**means:**
Promotion	doctorate / PhD He's writing a thesis on laser interferometry for his PhD.
promotion	*Beförderung; Werbeaktion*
proper	neat / tidy Do you always keep your workspace this tidy? Mine looks like a bomb has hit it.
proper	*anständig; angemessen*
Prospekt	brochure Can I give you one of our brochures? There is a price list at the back.
prospect	*Aussicht; potentieller Kunde*
Protokoll	minutes (of a meeting) Who's taking the minutes today?
protocol	*Verhaltensprotokoll; Plan*
Provision	commission We get paid on a commission basis: 10% of all sales.
provision	*Bereitstellung; Rücklage*

If you mean... This...	say this: means:
Prozess	trial The public were not allowed to spectate at the trial. But: We must improve our working processes if we are to become more competitive.
process	*Prozess*
prüfen	to examine / to test When we interview the candidates today we need to test their English on the spot.
prove	*beweisen*
Publikum	audience Our audience seems very attentive today, don't you think?
public	*Öffentlichkeit*
Pudding	custard / blancmange (BE) We often used to have blancmange at school for lunch. I hated it because it was always lumpy.
pudding	*Nachspeise*
punktuell	point by point Let me give you a point-by-point summary of the negotiation.
punctual	*pünktlich*

If you mean...	say this:
This...	**means:**
Quote	quota / share Our exports are unfortunately limited. If we exceed our quota, we can be fined.
quote	*Zitat*
raffiniert	sophisticated / ingenious This is an incredibly sophisticated piece of machinery. But: We don't use refined sugar; only raw cane.
refined	*veredelt; raffiniert*
rasch	rapid / swift I had to make a swift decision.
rash	*vorschnell*
Rasse	breed You have three dogs? Wow! What breed are they? But: We welcome people of all races, beliefs and abilities.
race	*Rasse; Rennen*

If you mean... / This...	say this: / means:
Rate	instalment We have agreed to allow this customer to pay in instalments. But: The current rate of inflation is quite worrying.
rate	*Kurs; Preis*
raten	to guess; to advise Can you guess what the next graph is going to show? I would advise you not to say anything just yet.
rate	*bewerten*
Ratio	rationale I want to know the rationale behind this decision.
ratio	*Verhältnis*
rationell	efficient(ly) This equipment enables the operator to clean all surfaces quickly and efficiently.
rational(ly)	*vernünftig*
reell	reasonable Is there a reasonable chance of our sales increasing this year?
real	*wirklich; echt*

If you mean... This...	say this: means:
Reklamation	complaint This department deals with customer complaints.
reclamation	*Rückgewinnung*
Rektor/in	head teacher /principal (AE) I need to leave the meeting early to go to my daughter's school for an appointment with the head teacher.
rector	*Pfarrer*
rentabel	viable / financially worthwhile We aren't sure if such an investment would be truly viable for our company.
rentable	*(ver)mietbar*
Rente	pension; annuity Have you thought about opening a savings account? You will need something to supplement the state pension. An annuity is a yearly payment of an allowance or income.
rent	*Miete*

If you mean... / This...	say this: / means:
repräsentativ	prestigious The consulting company has moved into some very prestigious new premises. But: These figures are not representative of the real situation.
representative	*charakteristisch*
Ressort	department He's in charge of the marketing department.
resort	*Ferienort; Ausweg*
Revision	audit; appeal I'm responsible for the internal audit. He's going to appeal against his court sentence.
revision	*Überarbeitung; Wiederholung (Lehrstoff)*
Rezept	recipe; prescription I know this amazing recipe for salmon lasagne. The doctor has given me a prescription for sleeping tablets.
receipt	*Quittung*

If you mean...	say this:
This...	**means:**
Rollen	wheels No, that's not my suitcase. Mine has wheels.
rolls	*Brötchen*
Roller	scooter My son has asked for a scooter with larger wheels for Christmas.
roller	*Lockenwickler*
Roman	novel I read two whole novels on the plane. It was a long flight!
roman	*Römer*
Rückseite	back / reverse You will find the instructions on the back of this card.
backside	*Hintern*
Salat	lettuce I love all kinds of lettuce but my favourites are romaine and iceberg. But: I only eat salad for lunch. I have to watch my waistline!
salad	*Salat*

If you mean...	say this:
This...	**means:**
sauer	angry Have you any idea why the boss is so angry? But: This cocktail is rather sour. I don't think I can finish it.
sour	*sauer*
scharf	spicy / hot How spicy would you like your curry? But: Be careful with those scissors; they are really sharp.
sharp	*scharf; scharfsinnig*
Schatten	shade It's 35 degrees in here. Is the air conditioning not working? But: The murderer was hiding in the shadows.
shadow	*Schatten*
Schema	pattern All of our marketing ideas seem to have followed the same pattern. Let's try something new this time.
scheme	*Programm; Plan; Intrige*
schreien	to shout I came to see who was shouting. What's the problem?
cry	*weinen*

If you mean... This...	say this: means:
schwimmen	to float The advantage of this material is that it floats on water. But: I always go for an early morning swim in the hotel pool when I'm on a business trip.
swim	schwimmen
See	lake The boss has invited us to go fishing with him on a nearby lake at the weekend.
sea	Meer
selbstbewusst	confident She's a confident person. She'll go far.
self-conscious	*gehemmt*
senden	to broadcast; to despatch A recorded interview with the president will be broadcast on all channels this evening. We'll despatch the goods to you immediately.
send	*schicken; versenden*

If you mean... This...	say this: means:
Sender	radio station; TV channel; transmitter All of the radio stations and TV channels are interested in reporting about our new product. There may be some public opposition to the location of this transmitter.
sender	*Absender*
sensibel	sensitive Be careful when voicing your opinions to Charles; he's very sensitive.
sensible	*vernünftig*
seriös	legitimate Can you confirm that you received a legitimate offer for this car?
serious	*ernst(haft)*
skrupellos	unscrupulous We will not do business with any unscrupulous partners. Everything must be above board.
scrupulous	*peinlich genau*
skurril	quirky / bizarre I agree; he's quite a bizarre character. He does an excellent job though.
scurrilous	*gemein; ordinär*

If you mean...	say this:
This...	**means:**
Slip	briefs (men and women); underpants (men); panties (women) My luggage hasn't arrived. I need to know the nearest place where I can buy briefs and shaving things.
slip	*Unterrock; Zettel*
Slipper	loafers / casual shoes Have you seen my loafers? I need to pack a pair for the time off in between meetings.
slipper	*Hauschuh / Pantoffel*
Smoking	dinner jacket (BE) / tuxedo (AE) Do I need to wear a dinner jacket this evening?
smoking	*Rauchen*
Soße	gravy Could we please have some more gravy for the beef? But: What type of sauce would you like with your burger – sweet and sour or hot chilli?
sauce	*Soße*

If you mean... / This...	say this: / means:
souverän	confident I have to say I was impressed by how confident you were when you gave your presentation today.
sovereign	*hoheitlich*
sparen	to save We can save at least 5% if we change suppliers now. But: Please, spare me the details. I get the idea.
spare	*verschonen*
spenden	to donate We have decided not to send Christmas cards this year. We will be donating money to charity instead.
spend	*ausgeben*
spendieren	to treat sb. to sth. Congratulations everybody, we've won the contract! Let's go the pub so I can treat you all to a drink.
spend	*ausgeben*

If you mean...	say this:
This...	**means:**
Spot	TV commercial / advert We've managed to get a local celebrity to appear in our commercial.
spot	*Pickel; Fleck; Ort / Stelle*
Sprecher	spokesperson A former colleague of mine has just become spokesperson for one of the major energy supply companies. But: We have invited a speaker today who is an expert in this field. I'd like you to give a big welcome to ...
speaker	*Redner; Sprecher*
springen	to jump; to run I would say that's a good reason to jump for joy, wouldn't you? I have to run over to the canteen again; I forgot to pick up my mobile when we left.
spring, to ~ sb.	jdn. (z.B. aus dem Gefängnis) rausholen
Stadium	stage / phase The product is still at the development stage.
stadium	*Stadion*

If you mean... This...	say this: means:
stark	strong I need someone strong to help me carry these boxes.
stark	*krass / schier*
starten	to take off; to launch We are sorry for the delay in taking off this morning. The rocket was launched punctually at 5am local time.
start	*beginnen*
Station	ward; stop She'll be staying in the maternity ward until Saturday. All exit the train! This is the final stop.
station	*Bahnhof; Stelle*
stationär	in hospital He's being treated in hospital for exhaustion. But: All traffic is stationary due to an accident.
stationary	*stehend; stationär*

If you mean... This...	say this: means:
stickig	stuffy Can we open some windows? It's so stuffy in here.
sticky	*klebrig*
Stock	floor; stick / cane Our offices are on the 25th floor. Since he broke his leg he's needed to use a stick to walk.
stock	*Inventar / Lagerbestand; Aktien*
Stoff	fabric; substance; topic We manufacture high-quality upholstery fabric. Our machines process a special type of material. This topic will provide plenty of discussion.
stuff	*Zeug*
streng	strict We have to follow very strict accounting procedures.
strong	*stark*
Studium	course (degree ~; at university / college)
study	*Untersuchung; Arbeitszimmer*

If you mean...	say this:
This...	**means:**
sympathisch	likeable She's a very likeable member of our team.
sympathetic	*mitfühlend*
Tablett	tray Do you know where we can find a tray to put all these champagne glasses on?
tablet	*Tablette*
Takt	interval; rhythm The train service runs in 30-minute intervals. I can't keep up with this rhythm. It's too fast! But: You need to show more tact when giving feedback.
tact	*Taktgefühl*
Tarif	charge / fee; scale Do you know what the fee is for translations of this type? We allocate pay increases to employees on the basis of the scales agreed with the trade unions.
tariff	*Zolltarif; Gebührenordnung*

If you mean...	say this:
This...	**means:**
Technik	technology Can you describe your company's technology to us in more detail? But: There is a special technique for doing this. Let me demonstrate it to you.
technique	*Methode / Vorgehensweise; Technik*
temperamentvoll	feisty / vivacious She's the most vivacious press agent we have ever had; she's so full of energy!
temperamental	*launisch; unzuverlässig*
terminieren	to schedule Can we schedule these meetings to take place every four weeks?
terminate	*beenden*
Thema	subject The subject of my presentation today is work-life balance. But: The theme surrounding the exhibition is 'light'.
theme	*Motiv; Titelsong*

If you mean...	say this:
This...	**means:**
These	theory Our managers support the theory that employee motivation cannot be increased only by offering more money.
thesis	*Dissertation; Doktorarbeit*
Tick	quirk He talks to himself while he's working. It's just one of his little quirks.
tick	*Zecke; Häkchen*
Tipp	bet It's a safe bet that we will get the contract. But: Have you got a tip for me on how to avoid spam?
tip	*Ratschlag; Trinkgeld; Tipp*
tippen	to type I'll come over to you as soon as I've finished typing this report.
tip	*ein Trinkgeld geben; kippen*
Transparent	banner I thought we could put up a few banners on our stand at the trade fair. They will draw more attention to us.
transparent	*durchsichtig; transparent*

If you mean... This...	say this: means:
treu	loyal They are a loyal customer. Please deal with their request without delay.
true	*wahr / echt*
Trubel	confusion; hubbub This decision is causing a lot of confusion among my colleagues. Why is there such a hubbub around here today? What's happened?
trouble	*Ärger; Unannehmlichkeiten*
überarbeiten	update / revise / amend These statistics are from last week. I will update them before we present to the board.
overwork	*sich überarbeiten*
überhören	to miss (hearing); to ignore (a remark) I'm sorry but I missed that. Could you re-peat it? I will ignore what you just said.
overhear	*zufällig hören*

If you mean... This...	say this: means:
übernehmen	to take over; to take on We are speculating that this company will take over at least one of its main competitors within the next year. Joanne will be taking on Silvia's responsibilities while she is on maternity leave.
overtake	*überholen*
übersehen	to miss (seeing) Oh, I'm sorry. I completely missed that part. I will finish translating it immediately.
oversee	*beaufsichtigen; überwachen*
Übersicht	overview Can you give us a short overview of the project?
oversight	*Versehen*
untergehen	to go down They failed to develop a good strategy. They're going to go down, mark my words.
undergo	*erfahren; sich unterziehen*
Unternehmer	entrepreneur / business owner
undertaker	*Leichenbestatter*

If you mean... This...	say this: means:
unter-schreiben	to sign As soon as the contract is signed we can proceed.
underwrite	*garantieren*
Ventilator	fan This office is too hot in summer. I need to get a fan for my desk.
ventilator	*Belüfter; Beatmungsgerät*
Visite	rounds The doctor will talk to you when he does his rounds later this morning.
visit	*Besuch*
Vokal	vowel The vowels are a, e, i, o and u.
vocal	*-Sänger; Gesang*
vorsehen	to budget; to set aside We have budgeted for a certain amount of bad debt. This money has been set aside for emergencies.
foresee	*vorhersehen*

If you mean... This...	say this: means:
wandern	to hike How about we take the whole department for a hike one weekend to boost morale?
wander	*umherwandern*
Warenhaus	department store If you need a souvenir, try looking in the department store in the main square.
warehouse	*Warenlager*
weil	because I want to go to the Budapest office because a face-to-face conversation will clear this problem up more effectively.
while	*während*
Werk	plant / works I'm going to the Manchester works this week, but I'll be back in London next Monday.
work	*Arbeit*
Weste	waistcoat (BE) / vest (AE)
vest	*Unterhemd (BE); Weste (AE)*
will	want I want to show you how this will work.
will	*werde / wirst / wird / werden / werdet*

If you mean...	say this:
This...	**means:**
winken	to wave Can you wave the waiter over if you catch his eye?
wink	*zwinkern*
Wunder	miracle It's a miracle that we managed to survive the economic problems. But: Can you name all seven wonders of the world?
wonder	*etw. verwunderliches*
wundern	to be surprised I'm surprised that you don't have jetlag. Do you never suffer from it?
wonder	*sich fragen*
Zensur	grade; censorship I got a satisfactory grade in the interim exam. The film has caused some criticism and is currently undergoing the censorship process.
censure	*Kritik*

If you mean... This...	say this: means:
Zylinder	top hat Do all men wear top hats at English weddings? But: The gas is stored in cylinders.
cylinder	*Zylinder*

Appendix

False friends game

If you would like to test how much you can remember from reading this book, try the false friends game below. It is a maze, also known as a labyrinth, but with text, and with options to choose from – some of which contain false friends.

Start by reading the text in box number 1, make your decision and then go to the next box that is mentioned. For example: you read box number 1 and decide for the second option. It says 'Go to 9', so continue reading at box number 9 and carry on until you are out of the maze.

1 It is Monday morning and a colleague from South Africa has come to Munich for a week to learn about your company and its administration processes. She will then return to SA to start her job there. You welcome her at reception and say to her

"Follow me and I'll introduce you to everyone in the bureau." **Go to 5.**

"Let me bring you to meet my chef." **Go to 9.**

"Come and meet my colleagues. We have all been looking forward to your arrival." **Go to 2.**

11 It is now Wednesday and you and your partner are having dinner with Karen in the city centre. You want to ensure that she enjoys her time in Munich. During the conversation, Karen asks you what you do in your spare time. You answer

"I make a lot of sport – cycling, running and wandering." **Go to 8.**

"I like going out into the nature – every weekend if possible." **Go to 12.**

"I play the clarinet in a small orchestra and I love badminton." **Go to 14.**

10 Karen is surprised. It is a bit early in the day for cakes, and she cannot see any on the table, only biscuits/cookies. The meeting starts and Karen is looking forward to learning a lot his week. **Go to 7.**

2 There is a staff meeting every Monday morning and you introduce Karen to colleagues. Afterwards, you say

"I'm responsible for the minutes, so excuse me a moment while I just get organized." **Go to 7.**

"Would you like some coffee and cakes?" **Go to 10.**

"I normally write the protocol for this meeting. Shall we sit at the front?" **Go to 4.**

12 The correct way to say *ich bin gern draußen in der Natur* is 'I like being outdoors' or 'I like spending time in the countryside.' **Go to 14.**

16 Congratulations, you have survived the week with an English-speaking visitor! If you made any mistakes at any time with false friends, make a note of them for future reference.

15 If someone has to amuse themselves, then it is because their host has no time for them – *sich selbst beschäftigen*. The right thing to say is 'I hope you enjoyed yourself here this week.' **Go to 16.**

9 Karen thinks you have your own personal *Chefkoch*. Whoops! Besides this, if you are moving something or someone to a destination further away from your current location, you 'take' it or them. So the correct thing to say was "Let me take you to meet my boss." **Go to 2.**

3 Karen doesn't understand. You have told her that she could be lucky at her new desk (*sie könnte dort Schwein haben*) and she doesn't know why. **Go to 11.**

13 Karen is smiling. A coffer is a large box for holding money, jewels and other treasures, normally something that pirates search for. It is an old-fashioned word. Nowadays, you might hear people use it in the context of the 'state coffers' – *die Staatskassen*. **Go to 16.**

14 Friday has arrived. Karen is departing in a few minutes and is waiting for a taxi to take her to the airport. You say

"It was nice to meet you, Karen. I hope you will call us if you have any questions when you are back in South Africa." **Go to 16.**

"Where is your coffer? You mustn't forget it! I hope we see us again soon. Goodbye!" **Go to 13.**

"I hope you amused yourself this week. Have a good journey home!" **Go to 15.**

8 It is that common problem that German speakers have with the verb *machen*. It is correct to say 'I do a lot of sports.' If you say you like wandering, you are saying *ich wandere gern herum*, but if you mean you like walking in the hills and mountains, say 'I like hiking.' **Go to 14.**

4 Karen is a little confused. You said you write the protocol but this sounds to her like you are responsible for the *Benimmregeln* for the meeting. **Go to 7.**

5 *Büro* is 'office' in English. It was a small mistake. You take your visitor, Karen, to meet the people she will be having more contact with in future. **Go to 2.**

6 Karen goes red. She suspects you saw her looking at Dan. He is a good-looking man, but he is wearing a wedding ring and she does not want a date with him, but she does have to make an appointment to talk with him about finance matters. And what is his job? Controller? Who does he control (*wen steuert er*)? **Go to 11.**

7 While you write the minutes (*Protokoll führen*) Karen agrees on some days and times to go to the other colleagues to learn about their areas of responsibility and their tasks. You ask Karen

"Have you a date with Dan, our controller, too? **Go to 6.**

This meeting finishes at 11 o'clock. I'll show you to your desk after that." **Go to 11.**

"After this meeting I'll show you where you can work this week. I'm sure you'll be lucky there. **Go to 3.**

English around the world

This TaschenGuide has been written in British English. In the explanations of the false friends there are references to American English terms if they vary from their English counterparts. Here are some useful general points to note:

- British English allows the use of 's' and 'z' in the spelling of some words, such as 'organise' or 'organize'. American English uses only 'z'.
- When you are writing any kind of correspondence on your computer, you can set the regional and language options in your word processing software to British English, American English, Indian English, Canadian English, or whatever you need at the time.
- Spelling- and grammar-checking extras also offer you the choice of using different versions of English.
- When communicating verbally in English to native speakers, you cannot expect to be corrected by your conversation partner. Even if you ask him or her to correct you, they will probably not do so, either out of politeness, or because they do not want to interrupt the flow of conversation. Watch their faces carefully for signs that they have not understood you, and if in doubt, ask.
- Learning false friends is the same as learning new vocabulary, but with the added importance of avoiding bigger misunderstandings.

Here are some practical tips for helping you to memorize new words and phrases:

If you see standard phrases in emails from other people that you want to use in your own correspondence, copy the sentences and paste them into a list. When you need them, you can copy them and paste them into your own emails or other documents.

Write new words and phrases onto sticky notes and put them on your bathroom mirror, your fridge, or a place that you look at frequently – perhaps your car dashboard, as long as it does not obstruct your concentration while driving! You will see the vocabulary again and again when you brush your teeth, are standing at your favourite place in the kitchen or driving to and from work.

Internet resources

You can increase your knowledge of false friends by confronting yourself with them often. Here are some websites on which you will find more information about false friends:

www.business-english.de/false_friends_quiz.html
provides you with a test of your knowledge of general false friends.

www.business-english.de/quiz/false_friend_contr/
contains questions specifically for business English.

http://en.wikipedia.org/wiki/False_friend
has much more background information about the subject of false friends and deals with other foreign languages, not just German.

www.englisch-hilfen.de/words/false_friends.htm
offers a comprehensive, tabular list of false friends.

www.bbc.co.uk/languages/yoursay/false_friends/german/mist_common_false_friends_in_german_englishgerman.shtml
This BBC webpage has some amusing contributions from its readers.

The above-mentioned Internet addresses were correct at the time of going to press. The author is not responsible for the content or availability of these sites.

Bibliografische Information der Deutschen Nationalbibliothek

Die Deutsche Nationalbibliothek verzeichnet diese Publikation in der Deutschen Nationalbibliografie; detaillierte bibliografische Daten sind im Internet über http://dnb.d-nb.de abrufbar.

ISBN 978-3-448-01113-3
Bestell-Nr. 00364-0001

Redaktionsanschrift: Fraunhoferstraße 5, 82152 Planegg
Fon: (0 89) 8 95 17-0, Fax: (0 89) 8 95 17-2 50
E-Mail: online@haufe.de
Internet www.haufe.de
Redaktion: Jürgen Fischer

Konzeption und Realisation: Sylvia Rein, 81371 München
Lektorat: Lesley Engel, 83674 Gaißach
Umschlaggestaltung: Kienle gestaltet, 70178 Stuttgart
Druck: freiburger graphische betriebe, 79108 Freiburg

Zur Herstellung der Bücher wird nur alterungsbeständiges Papier verwendet.

Die Autorin

Stephanie Shellabear

ist selbständige Englisch-Trainerin, Übersetzerin und Korrektorin. Nach ihrem Studium der Betriebswirtschaft und Deutsch in Großbritannien war sie zehn Jahre lang im Bereich Finanzen und Rechnungswesen bei einer renommierten Unternehmensberatung in München tätig sowie einige Jahre am Münchener Sitz eines globalen Computer-Herstellers.

Weiterführende Literatur

„Die besten Bewerbungsmuster Englisch", von Lisa Förster, 176 Seiten, mit CD-ROM, € 19,80.
ISBN 978-3-448-08781-9, Bestell-Nr. 04078

„business-english Trainer. Optimale Unterstützung für ein perfektes Englisch in Ihrem Job", PDF-Newsletter, 9 Seiten pro Ausgabe, 12 Ausgaben pro Jahr und zusätzlich 12 Monate Zugang auf die Professional-Inhalte von www.business-english.de, € 106,80. ISBN 978-3-8092-1985-9, Bestell-Nr. 00839VJ